AF815600

MY CHECK REGISTER

MANAGE AND KEEP TRACK OF YOUR BANKING TRANSACTIONS

Wide Edition

CHECK REGISTER

NAME:____________________________________

PHONE: __________________________________

Debits, Checks, and Deposits

Starting Balance: ____________

Date	Trans Type/ Check No.	Description	Payment Debit (-)	Payment Credit (+)	Balance

Debits, Checks, and Deposits

Starting Balance: ______________

Date	Trans Type/ Check No.	Description	Payment Debit (-)		Payment Credit (+)		Balance	

Debits, Checks, and Deposits

Starting Balance: ______________

Date	Trans Type/ Check No.	Description	Payment Debit (-)		Payment Credit (+)		Balance	

Debits, Checks, and Deposits

Starting Balance: ______________

Date	Trans Type/ Check No.	Description	Payment Debit (-)		Payment Credit (+)		Balance	

Debits, Checks, and Deposits

Starting Balance: ____________

Date	Trans Type/ Check No.	Description	Payment Debit (-)	Payment Credit (+)	Balance

Debits, Checks, and Deposits

Starting Balance: ______________

Date	Trans Type/ Check No.	Description	Payment Debit (-)	Payment Credit (+)	Balance

Debits, Checks, and Deposits **Starting Balance:** ______________

Date	Trans Type/ Check No.	Description	Payment Debit (-)		Payment Credit (+)		Balance	

Debits, Checks, and Deposits

Starting Balance: ______________

Date	Trans Type/ Check No.	Description	Payment Debit (-)		Payment Credit (+)		Balance	

Debits, Checks, and Deposits

Starting Balance: ____________

Date	Trans Type/ Check No.	Description	Payment Debit (-)	Payment Credit (+)	Balance

Debits, Checks, and Deposits

Starting Balance: ______________

Date	Trans Type/ Check No.	Description	Payment Debit (-)	Payment Credit (+)	Balance

Debits, Checks, and Deposits

Starting Balance: ____________

Date	Trans Type/ Check No.	Description	Payment Debit (-)	Payment Credit (+)	Balance

Debits, Checks, and Deposits

Starting Balance: ______________

Date	Trans Type/ Check No.	Description	Payment Debit (-)		Payment Credit (+)		Balance	

Debits, Checks, and Deposits

Starting Balance: ______________

Date	Trans Type/ Check No.	Description	Payment Debit (-)	Payment Credit (+)	Balance

Debits, Checks, and Deposits

Starting Balance: ______________

Date	Trans Type/ Check No.	Description	Payment Debit (-)		Payment Credit (+)		Balance	

Debits, Checks, and Deposits

Starting Balance: ____________

Date	Trans Type/ Check No.	Description	Payment Debit (-)		Payment Credit (+)		Balance	

Debits, Checks, and Deposits

Starting Balance: ____________

Date	Trans Type/ Check No.	Description	Payment Debit (-)		Payment Credit (+)		Balance	

Debits, Checks, and Deposits **Starting Balance:** ____________

Date	Trans Type/ Check No.	Description	Payment Debit (-)		Payment Credit (+)		Balance	

Debits, Checks, and Deposits

Starting Balance: ______________

Date	Trans Type/ Check No.	Description	Payment Debit (-)		Payment Credit (+)		Balance	

Debits, Checks, and Deposits

Starting Balance: ______________

Date	Trans Type/ Check No.	Description	Payment Debit (-)		Payment Credit (+)		Balance	

Debits, Checks, and Deposits **Starting Balance:** ______________

Date	Trans Type/ Check No.	Description	Payment Debit (-)		Payment Credit (+)		Balance	

Debits, Checks, and Deposits

Starting Balance: ______________

Date	Trans Type/ Check No.	Description	Payment Debit (-)	Payment Credit (+)	Balance

Debits, Checks, and Deposits

Starting Balance: ______________

Date	Trans Type/ Check No.	Description	Payment Debit (-)		Payment Credit (+)		Balance	

Debits, Checks, and Deposits

Starting Balance: ____________

Date	Trans Type/ Check No.	Description	Payment Debit (-)	Payment Credit (+)	Balance

Debits, Checks, and Deposits

Starting Balance: ______________

Date	Trans Type/ Check No.	Description	Payment Debit (-)		Payment Credit (+)		Balance	

Debits, Checks, and Deposits

Starting Balance: ____________

Date	Trans Type/ Check No.	Description	Payment Debit (-)	Payment Credit (+)	Balance

Debits, Checks, and Deposits

Starting Balance: ____________

Date	Trans Type/ Check No.	Description	Payment Debit (-)		Payment Credit (+)		Balance	

Debits, Checks, and Deposits

Starting Balance: ______________

Date	Trans Type/ Check No.	Description	Payment Debit (-)		Payment Credit (+)		Balance	

Debits, Checks, and Deposits

Starting Balance: ____________

Date	Trans Type/ Check No.	Description	Payment Debit (-)		Payment Credit (+)		Balance	

Debits, Checks, and Deposits

Starting Balance: ______________

Date	Trans Type/ Check No.	Description	Payment Debit (-)	Payment Credit (+)	Balance

Debits, Checks, and Deposits

Starting Balance: ____________

Date	Trans Type/ Check No.	Description	Payment Debit (-)		Payment Credit (+)		Balance	

Debits, Checks, and Deposits

Starting Balance: ____________

Date	Trans Type/ Check No.	Description	Payment Debit (-)	Payment Credit (+)	Balance

Debits, Checks, and Deposits

Starting Balance: ________________

Date	Trans Type/ Check No.	Description	Payment Debit (-)	Payment Credit (+)	Balance

Debits, Checks, and Deposits

Starting Balance: ______________

Date	Trans Type/ Check No.	Description	Payment Debit (-)	Payment Credit (+)	Balance

Debits, Checks, and Deposits

Starting Balance: ______________

Date	Trans Type/ Check No.	Description	Payment Debit (-)		Payment Credit (+)		Balance	

Debits, Checks, and Deposits

Starting Balance: ______________

Date	Trans Type/ Check No.	Description	Payment Debit (-)	Payment Credit (+)	Balance

Debits, Checks, and Deposits

Starting Balance: ______________

Date	Trans Type/ Check No.	Description	Payment Debit (-)		Payment Credit (+)		Balance	

Debits, Checks, and Deposits

Starting Balance: ______________

Date	Trans Type/ Check No.	Description	Payment Debit (-)	Payment Credit (+)	Balance

Debits, Checks, and Deposits

Starting Balance: ______________

Date	Trans Type/ Check No.	Description	Payment Debit (-)		Payment Credit (+)		Balance	

Debits, Checks, and Deposits

Starting Balance: ______________

Date	Trans Type/ Check No.	Description	Payment Debit (-)	Payment Credit (+)	Balance

Debits, Checks, and Deposits

Starting Balance: ______________

Date	Trans Type/ Check No.	Description	Payment Debit (-)		Payment Credit (+)		Balance	

Debits, Checks, and Deposits

Starting Balance: ______________

Date	Trans Type/ Check No.	Description	Payment Debit (-)		Payment Credit (+)		Balance	

Debits, Checks, and Deposits

Starting Balance: ________________

Date	Trans Type/ Check No.	Description	Payment Debit (-)		Payment Credit (+)		Balance	

Debits, Checks, and Deposits

Starting Balance: ______________

Date	Trans Type/ Check No.	Description	Payment Debit (-)	Payment Credit (+)	Balance

Debits, Checks, and Deposits

Starting Balance: ______________

Date	Trans Type/ Check No.	Description	Payment Debit (-)		Payment Credit (+)		Balance	

Debits, Checks, and Deposits

Starting Balance: ____________

Date	Trans Type/ Check No.	Description	Payment Debit (-)	Payment Credit (+)	Balance

Debits, Checks, and Deposits

Starting Balance: ____________

Date	Trans Type/ Check No.	Description	Payment Debit (-)		Payment Credit (+)		Balance	

Debits, Checks, and Deposits

Starting Balance: ____________

Date	Trans Type/ Check No.	Description	Payment Debit (-)	Payment Credit (+)	Balance

Debits, Checks, and Deposits

Starting Balance: ______________

Date	Trans Type/ Check No.	Description	Payment Debit (-)		Payment Credit (+)		Balance	

Debits, Checks, and Deposits

Starting Balance: ______________

Date	Trans Type/ Check No.	Description	Payment Debit (-)	Payment Credit (+)	Balance

Debits, Checks, and Deposits

Starting Balance: ______________

Date	Trans Type/ Check No.	Description	Payment Debit (-)	Payment Credit (+)	Balance

Debits, Checks, and Deposits

Starting Balance: ______________

Date	Trans Type/ Check No.	Description	Payment Debit (-)		Payment Credit (+)		Balance	

Debits, Checks, and Deposits

Starting Balance: ______________

Date	Trans Type/ Check No.	Description	Payment Debit (-)		Payment Credit (+)		Balance	

Debits, Checks, and Deposits

Starting Balance: ______________

Date	Trans Type/ Check No.	Description	Payment Debit (-)	Payment Credit (+)	Balance

Debits, Checks, and Deposits **Starting Balance:** ____________

Date	Trans Type/ Check No.	Description	Payment Debit (-)		Payment Credit (+)		Balance	

Debits, Checks, and Deposits

Starting Balance: ______________

Date	Trans Type/ Check No.	Description	Payment Debit (-)	Payment Credit (+)	Balance

Debits, Checks, and Deposits

Starting Balance: ________________

Date	Trans Type/ Check No.	Description	Payment Debit (-)	Payment Credit (+)	Balance

Debits, Checks, and Deposits

Starting Balance: ______________

Date	Trans Type/ Check No.	Description	Payment Debit (-)	Payment Credit (+)	Balance

Debits, Checks, and Deposits

Starting Balance: ________________

Date	Trans Type/ Check No.	Description	Payment Debit (-)		Payment Credit (+)		Balance	

Debits, Checks, and Deposits

Starting Balance: ______________

Date	Trans Type/ Check No.	Description	Payment Debit (-)	Payment Credit (+)	Balance

Debits, Checks, and Deposits

Starting Balance: ______________

Date	Trans Type/ Check No.	Description	Payment Debit (-)		Payment Credit (+)		Balance	

Debits, Checks, and Deposits

Starting Balance: ______________

Date	Trans Type/ Check No.	Description	Payment Debit (-)		Payment Credit (+)		Balance	

Debits, Checks, and Deposits

Starting Balance: ______________

Date	Trans Type/ Check No.	Description	Payment Debit (-)		Payment Credit (+)		Balance	

Debits, Checks, and Deposits **Starting Balance:** ______________

Date	Trans Type/ Check No.	Description	Payment Debit (-)		Payment Credit (+)		Balance	

Debits, Checks, and Deposits

Starting Balance: ____________

Date	Trans Type/ Check No.	Description	Payment Debit (-)		Payment Credit (+)		Balance	

Debits, Checks, and Deposits

Starting Balance: ____________

Date	Trans Type/ Check No.	Description	Payment Debit (-)		Payment Credit (+)		Balance	

Debits, Checks, and Deposits

Starting Balance: ______________

Date	Trans Type/ Check No.	Description	Payment Debit (-)	Payment Credit (+)	Balance

Debits, Checks, and Deposits Starting Balance: ____________

Date	Trans Type/ Check No.	Description	Payment Debit (-)	Payment Credit (+)	Balance

Debits, Checks, and Deposits

Starting Balance: ____________

Date	Trans Type/ Check No.	Description	Payment Debit (-)		Payment Credit (+)		Balance	

Debits, Checks, and Deposits

Starting Balance: ____________

Date	Trans Type/ Check No.	Description	Payment Debit (-)	Payment Credit (+)	Balance

Debits, Checks, and Deposits

Starting Balance: ______________

Date	Trans Type/ Check No.	Description	Payment Debit (-)		Payment Credit (+)		Balance	

Debits, Checks, and Deposits

Starting Balance: ______________

Date	Trans Type/ Check No.	Description	Payment Debit (-)	Payment Credit (+)	Balance

Debits, Checks, and Deposits

Starting Balance: ______________

Date	Trans Type/ Check No.	Description	Payment Debit (-)		Payment Credit (+)		Balance	

Debits, Checks, and Deposits

Starting Balance: ______________

Date	Trans Type/ Check No.	Description	Payment Debit (-)		Payment Credit (+)		Balance	

Debits, Checks, and Deposits **Starting Balance:** ____________

Date	Trans Type/ Check No.	Description	Payment Debit (-)		Payment Credit (+)		Balance	

Debits, Checks, and Deposits

Starting Balance: ____________

Date	Trans Type/ Check No.	Description	Payment Debit (-)	Payment Credit (+)	Balance

Debits, Checks, and Deposits

Starting Balance: ______________

Date	Trans Type/ Check No.	Description	Payment Debit (-)		Payment Credit (+)		Balance	

Debits, Checks, and Deposits

Starting Balance: ______________

Date	Trans Type/ Check No.	Description	Payment Debit (-)		Payment Credit (+)		Balance	

Debits, Checks, and Deposits

Starting Balance: ____________

Date	Trans Type/ Check No.	Description	Payment Debit (-)		Payment Credit (+)		Balance	

Debits, Checks, and Deposits

Starting Balance: ______________

Date	Trans Type/ Check No.	Description	Payment Debit (-)	Payment Credit (+)	Balance

Debits, Checks, and Deposits

Starting Balance: ________________

Date	Trans Type/ Check No.	Description	Payment Debit (-)		Payment Credit (+)		Balance	

Debits, Checks, and Deposits

Starting Balance: ____________

Date	Trans Type/ Check No.	Description	Payment Debit (-)		Payment Credit (+)		Balance	

Debits, Checks, and Deposits

Starting Balance: ____________

Date	Trans Type/ Check No.	Description	Payment Debit (-)		Payment Credit (+)		Balance	

Debits, Checks, and Deposits

Starting Balance: ______________

Date	Trans Type/ Check No.	Description	Payment Debit (-)		Payment Credit (+)		Balance	

Debits, Checks, and Deposits

Starting Balance: ______________

Date	Trans Type/ Check No.	Description	Payment Debit (-)		Payment Credit (+)		Balance	

Debits, Checks, and Deposits

Starting Balance: ______________

Date	Trans Type/ Check No.	Description	Payment Debit (-)		Payment Credit (+)		Balance	

Debits, Checks, and Deposits

Starting Balance: ________________

Date	Trans Type/ Check No.	Description	Payment Debit (-)		Payment Credit (+)		Balance	

Debits, Checks, and Deposits

Starting Balance: ____________

Date	Trans Type/ Check No.	Description	Payment Debit (-)	Payment Credit (+)	Balance

Made in United States
Orlando, FL
04 November 2026

90204242R00050